LIVING MONEY BOUND

Growth Action Thinking

SEGUNDO Pérez

Copyright © 2014 by Segundo Ramón Pérez

All rights reserved.

ISBN: 10: 0692500219
ISBN-13: 978-0-692-50021-7

DEDICATION

Written for you!
Devoted to those who aspire to achieve.
Dedicated especially to your search for happiness and future success.

CONTENTS

	Acknowledgments	i
	Introduction	1
1	LIFE'S CASH DILEMMAS	7
	Personal Revenue Production Is More Than Just Money	
1.1	Mirthful Money?	8
1.2	Stewardship = Your Economic Situation	11
1.3	Prosperity Gets Away Every Day I Wait to Serve	16
2	REVELATIONS OF AFFLUENCE	26
	Holistic Rewards After a New "Personal Baseline"	
2.1	Should We Let Losers Help Us Fail?	27
2.2	The Most Effective, Loving Money Fund Manager	31
2.3	The Goodness of Money	37
3	A JOYFUL PROSPEROUS LIFE	41
	Receive the Empowerment of Prosperity	
3.1	GAT: The Three Phases To Empowered Prosperity	42
3.2	Money Working For You 24 Hours A Day	55
3.3	Assuring Living Well!	64

ACKNOWLEDGMENTS

To the amazing women and men in my life -
Olivia, the best Daughter and Rachele Honey, the best wife; mi Madre Caridad, mi Padre Ramón, Julia and Josefina, my honorable grandmothers; Luis Martinez, mentor and Dr. Cheulho Lee, my financial professors.

It is because of your unified efforts I have enjoyed a wonderful life, and understand the needs for opportunity among all immigrants who seek an affluent life in the United States of America. The result of this experience serves as personal knowledge to help our community. Living Money Bound is about living out my dream through service to God's people.

Thank You

INTRODUCTION

Success seems elusive, especially when it comes to money. Dreams are often out of financial reach. Solutions to making financial dreams a reality seem doable but can be time consuming, costly, and a lot of additional work. A group of successful people follow a simple way of thinking about personal growth. They also implement simple concepts.

It is easy to overlook our daily development as a growing, living organism. Continuous growth is usually associated with babies and toddlers. We can see their rapid physical and mental growth develop daily in front of our eyes. Teenagers are also bunched up in a group, as if all develop and think the same with misguided rebel thoughts. We on the other hand, the individuals of twenty something plus are stressed-out. Overworked-weekend-yearning moms and men tend to neglect personal growth. The disillusioned forty-plus crowd forgets the natural capacities to adjust prosperous behaviors over time.

If we are honest with ourselves and demand self-acceptance, we can realize that to operate successfully we need to move forward to our next level in life. Taking this pivotal first step however, results in posing some thought provoking questions. Was the "old school" thinking working for me? Why not? How do I process reality now? Have my dreams changed? How so? How do I get my dream to become a living joyful reality? Are there actions that will lead to the fulfillment of my dream on my terms and not someone else's? And above all, where do I start? The answers forwarded on this path to financial enlightenment rest in this book's methodology:

- Honest self-exploration of life style in need of betterment;
- Positive results caused by easy to comprehend explanations;
- Concepts reinforced by real-world activities.

I like to call the concept <u>Growth Action Thinking</u> (GAT).

The interactive design of this book continues by taking you through a series of life stories showcasing people who faced our similar circumstances. Everyone at some point needs to assess the actions necessary to overcome financial frustration. People succeed in areas that they are lacking through remembering simple concepts to help them. Some of the inquisitive stories deal with the relationships among money to spiritual empowerment, recovery of health, or the repair of certain family interactions. Detailed personality stories deal with the laying down of personal shame caused by lack of money. Finally, envisioning stories bring all personal financial aspects together as we become motivated to discuss the failure of having yet achieved personal goals. These are just some of the important areas of interest in this book.

Simple ideas are often viewed as tools of least value. The reality of simple ideas is that they can help us gain a favorable position. GAT is an unconditionally useful concept in repositioning. It keeps things simple by making ideas and plans easy to understand. Ultimately, GAT proves itself highly beneficial for those seeking financial happiness because it survives the ages time and time again.

The problem of transporting large quantities or heavy objects, for example, sets the perfect opportunity for requiring a simple solution: how do we effectively move a large load with the least amount of effort? Place the load on top of anything that rolls or floats. An ancient person dreamed up this simple idea, to manufacture trees into rolling wheels and floating ships. Today the same idea has advanced into riding on steel wheels or where large shipments of crude oil are transported daily by sea on metal tankers. We are consequently not newborns to simple successful ideas. Martin Luther King, Jr., Jose Marti, Toussaint L'Ouverture, Simon Bolivar, George Washington, Benjamin Franklin, and Abraham Lincoln were all attuned to the same thinking: to perpetrate positive continuous growth results in the advancing of our personal states and the securing of brighter futures.

Success is about bringing fresh direction to complex ideas so that they become simpler doable actions. Another example in simplicity is to make extra money by investing in natural energy transport stocks. Do it in the style of guerilla warfare. Enter when it is good and then get out when the market fluctuates negatively in relationship to your preset financial criteria, simple. The true simplicity in making money is revealed by reducing the supposed complexity behind it. Subsequently, another option is offering the right service to the right person with the right need. When we select such moneymaking activities like investments, entrepreneurship, or corporate leadership for the first time and understand how to react with enhanced self-supportive thinking *that* is simplicity in action. This is a hallmark for success. When we produce the extra cash for what we want to accomplish it is, simply, freedom.

> STOP an everyday struggle by maintaining a homage to personal history which may no longer fit the current economic positions.
>
> STOP pushing success away by artificially complicating a good simple idea.

Outcome Action Thinking Seminar **(OATS)**.

All the Simple Ideas That We Need to Reach Levels Above

OATS IS FINANCIAL NOURISHMENT.

Living Money Bound explores ways of optimal personal and financial success by adjusting our relationship with finances through the use of simple ideas. The public, regardless of education or background, can understand the concept of moving forward through personal growth by taking actions based on simple financial ideas, inclusive of Christian living. *Stewardships committed to spreading the Kingdom of God, by growing spiritually can transform our lives, and the lives of those around us.* As a general observation, these individuals who practice stewardship tend to become quite successful in their own rights. Understanding this general simplicity concept model and accepting its use is key in ending your financial frustrations. Whether a person is religiously observant, or starting out on such a path, one can finally satisfy the urge to climb for a better job or that desire to open a business.

I have had the triple privilege of serving as a business teacher in academia, a business consultant to industry, and a motivator for individuals searching for personal and business equilibrium. My focus as an author is to motivate you, the reader, to perform simple actions which will empower you to seek and reach the next level in your financial life.

Change by any great degree is based on self-ownership and the routine practical application of new simple ideas. People may have different financial needs, but everyone innately has a certain level of basic business understanding. It is all they need to clearly reach their new goals using GAT. Years of formal study, experience, and daily practical application have contributed to the formation of the Growth Action Thinking (GAT) model. These principles have come from my own life. It is my passion that you are motivated by the reading of this book to reach your own financial equilibrium.

Everyone has suffered some type of debilitating difficulty during the last sequence of global economic troubles, which required rapid substantial personal changes, myself included. The survivors and more importantly, the winners are those people whose preparation and understanding of personal financial basics set them aside from the rest. Do we need to wait until the next financial crisis to begin personal financial management?

The aftermath of just reading <u>Living Money Bound</u> may not lead to a clearly definable economic change for you or your family. You may need to re-read, question, process, and reflect on all the content in this book in order to reach a daily functional understanding and acceptance of the main concept of simplicity. Economic lifestyles become engraved in our brain just like our beliefs in political parties or religion. All different beliefs serve the purpose of financial survival. I think we can all agree that the levels of lifestyles are different for the haves and the have-nots. Background, family, education, emotions, economic opportunity, religion, and as empirical data suggests, gender as well sets a life-long pattern for our levels of financial independence. However, politicians can change political affiliations, and people change their religions. Consequently, let us try to become motivated enough to change our financial standing. One proven way is by thinking of simple actions. The end of our financial frustrations, satisfy the urge to climb for that better job, or open our business is under personal control.

Financial survival can be frightening to the point of total functional shutdown. We tend to call it "working hard for a day's pay" and getting paid just enough to almost avoid bankruptcy. The notion that most people can generate personal financial growth above any current level becomes unbelievable. Skeptics may at times undervalue the effectiveness of discussion, advocating personal financial gains primarily from a motivational point of view rather than affirming a technical or quantitative methodology.

Thus, I recognize as well the need for practical financial training of our population. The harm done by a lack of personal business knowledge, and an endless desire to spend money can only be resolved by motivating the masses. It is time to take actions toward stabilizing personal financial outlook. Yes, the purpose of this book is to motivate! However, this book is also accompanied by a series of self-help financial workshops, dedicated to the needs of the average person's financial independence, and as heads of the household. First, "Life's Cash Flow Dilemmas" includes chapters as a platform for personal and financial analysis, regarding personal revenue or the lack thereof on top of setting a baseline for growth. "Revelations of Affluence" follows the preparation and receiving of revenue from this new personal baseline. Finally, "A Joyful Prosperous Life" finalizes your transformation with an evaluation for how Growth Action Thinking can work for you. It includes the three phases to GAT empowerment. It is a great tool for anyone who likes hands-on practical learning.

Another way of getting benefits from the <u>Living Money Bound</u> is with the use of the MS PowerPoint and Apple Key Notes presentations for a multi-visual self-review. They are for people or educational groups who prefer to see an interactive show using media and technology. I also pass on the money knowledge by offering engaging web talks in which group help is available or even individual mentoring.

Motivation, dedication to the ultimate goal, and baby steps are the keys to personal financial stability through the use of GAT's simple ideas. I invite you to share in the excitement embraced by this servant and personal business educator. Together let us motivate you to a higher personal level of enjoying monetary freedom. Regardless of present position, <u>Living Money Bound</u> remains my personal hope and encouragement regarding the mission of using proven simple ideas, as tools to gain respectful revenue in the course of life. Escape the everyday! Enter the world where affluence is attainable as a reality. Failure embraces those who do not dare committing to success in their lives. Motivation is the key, followed by knowledge, then action towards your objective. Enjoy the book, learn, get motivated, and pass it on in the joy of prosperity. Let the skeptics stay as non-believers. Follow your dreams.

1

LIFE'S CASH DILEMMAS

Personal Revenue Production Is More Than Just Money

CHAPTER 1.1

MIRTHFUL MONEY?

Let us dare to apply ballpark statistics to a simple theory that a majority of Americans do not understand: "*mirth, themselves, nor money*". Everyone knows money and understands it at some level, or at least we like to think so. Self-knowledge after a few years of adulthood helps us evolve psychologically enough to regulate, how, when, and on whom we spend our money. In addition, survival skills hone in on our abilities as mind power manages over earthly problems. It is a positive money-person relationship that makes us happier. We are able to identify problems and understand the support of money leads to resolutions. The only mystery to resolve in the "*mirth and money*" concept: is the word "*mirth.*" Do you honestly understand what I mean by *mirth*? If you know the meaning of mirth then you can just skip the next two sentences. However, if any misunderstanding exists in your mind as to its meaning and grammatical use, then read on.

Mirth, according to Webster's dictionary is plainly stated as meaning "full of gladness; showing high spirited merriment or cheerfulness". It demonstrates a language that is not commonly practiced by the Urban Juanita. People no longer go around saying "*mirth* this" or "mirth that" we simply say cheerfulness. Therefore, the "*mirth and money*" connection has no mystery, right? Mirth, as it relates to ourselves and money then, essentially means that when we earn extra money from investments, entrepreneurship or corporate leadership we are happier.

The proper knowledge of financial terms is extremely important for successful personal business financiers. The ability to use economic opportunities for personal gain is similar to riding public transportation. Each bus, subway, or commuter train has a set destination. All we do when desiring to go from point A to point B is to have a map or app, learn the route's destination, and know where we're going. Investing, opening a small business, obtaining a business degree, passing a state professional licensing test, or putting our financial situations in order can be accomplished using similar practices. An individual sees a need for greater income. The astute person sets out to learn all about getting it. I must confess that following sports statistics seems more difficult than following economic trends. Why? Because I have never taken the time to relate what I know to sports statistics.

Joseph's interpretation of the Pharaoh's dream details a practice conducted by the ancient ruling class of using advisors. Successful persons of any era do not think in isolation. As a step in the decision-making process, perceived experts broadcast their knowledge of interpretations and ideas to the ruler and the elite courts. In Joseph's case, he explains to Pharaoh that his dream of "seven fat and well-formed cows coming up from the Nile" is symbolic of prosperity [Gen: 41:1- 43]. For us, it means "a bull market", "in the money", or an "upswing in the reporting cycle".

KNOWLEDGE IS WHAT MAKES KINGS OUT OF MERE MORTALS IN THE BUSINESS WORLD! Professional money managers, stock brokers, business advisors, certified public accountants (CPA), business news broadcasters, lawyers, and the scriptures are extremely helpful in providing expert information for our decision-making. This financial decision-making process constitutes researching issues before putting the capital to work. We do not "buy on a whim"! We don't just take Aunt Tillie's "word for it"! The primary goal from having a decision-making process is to lower the possibility of any losses to less than one. As well, the primary reason to use professional expert investment knowledge is to produce a constant return on our investments. I do not believe in losing money... Do you?

Addendum: Now, with all that new money, how are expenditures going to echo personal devotion to serve, follow, and live a life of spiritual faith? A person in true prosperity is to still remain a poor widow in our stewardship life (Mark 12: 41-44) rather than exist only as a rich man (Mark 10:17-31). Prosperity as a flourishing of good fortune, success, and all the joyful moments of life can only be real when accomplished in faith and irrevocable partnership with Jesus Christ.

CHAPTER 1.2

STEWARDSHIP = YOUR ECONOMIC SITUATION

The **effects** of poverty overwhelm people without money. Low wages encourages those who strive for financial security to seek more money. Sergio, a Venezuelan friend of mine from the music ministry at my church appears financially comfortable. The guy recently gained the asset value of two apartment buildings, filled with section 8 renters. He boasts a 1.5% vacancy factor in neighborhoods where seasoned independent landlords are lucky to operate at 6% vacancy. Corporate landlords in the area stipulate 9% vacancy in their pro-forma million dollar budgets. While down the street, a married couple loses a duplex to foreclosure.

Ignore the economic trends. It's bad for everyone in some comparative form, one way or the other during any given time. What we need to concentrate on is the individual mindset of each landlord sharing the same neighborhood who are creating different outcomes for each of their operations.

Sergio is both a dreamer AND a doer. He is not a time wasting over thinker. He is fast and furious in his financial decisions. He does not procrastinate. His actions are completely concentrated on his expected outcome. His father relates that Sergio was driven and focused in the "old unstable country". Sergio confesses that he took a high risk in buying the buildings during a downturned economy. It was the only time when the prices were low enough for him to afford the down payment. He signed on a large mortgage at a low interest rate. He managed to reduce expenses from the gross rent and ended up with a 12% profit. This is a prime example of guidance through the mindset of <u>Growth Action Thinking Outcomes</u> (GATO). Sergio's outcome in vacancies must be 1.5% or better. He has a rental plan full of interesting options. He can rent an apartment within ten days of notice of a renter vacating the premises. On the other hand, the corporate staffers earning a steady salary do not care how fast a new renter moves leading into undue losses. The married couple were too preoccupied worrying about getting the "right renter". They lost focus of the reasons they bought the property in the first place.

Sergio's key to success rests on outcome driven actions: striving for the security of money plus focusing on stewardship. He knows exactly what he wants. Maybe it took some reflection for a period of time, but the young immigrant desiring to become a profitable landlord, while, also satisfying acts of service ultimately explained to himself that the outcome should look and feel a certain way. This is the core of the GAT principles of outcome. The exercise of searching for outcomes plus generating a decisive selection of said outcomes, naturally brings simple ideas to our minds on how to become more secure. In Sergio's case it matters not what he does. It only matters that his actions lead toward financial security.

- What is it that we want to do?
- Can we explain our deep desire <u>at this moment</u> to reach a particular position in our life?

Stop reading! Take the time to answer these last two questions on a sheet of paper, tablet or cellphone's note pad.

Inspirations are heavenly sent moments to open the windows of our minds to simple, positive, creative ideas. Seven years ago, I started to make a left turn at 103rd Street from the ramp off the Palmetto expressway in Hialeah, Florida. It was on the way to school where I was a business and finance teacher. Day three of my first year

I saw a beggar, and donated a dollar and a rosary, asking her to pray for us both. The person appeared astonished, smiling and walking away never even muttering a polite thank you. About a week later I gave the same person a buck but this time with no rosary or request for mutual, eternal salvation. She unexpectedly thanked me with what appeared to be a true hearted welcoming of my stewardship. The sense of a person in need and a person willing to help appeared to come across to us both as a simple idea for hope.

We now know each other. Our eyes from time to time meet at that street corner, when she is in town to escape the north during its fierce winter months. I think this person is meant to inspire me to believe even stronger in the gifts that God has given me daily. One of those gifts is as a servant in helping people to better their financial lives. That person at the corner has a God given place in the scheme of things at this moment: for all of us to give and receive Divine Services. We ALL have a place in the divine scheme of things. Our stewardship may manifest in different ways. Honor Our Maker. Honor our lives with simple quality stewardship both in giving alms and receiving grace. One of the most amazing outcomes of inspired stewardship is that the finances seem to just take care of themselves.

A strategic action is to begin with keeping stewardship fresh in your mind as a part of the decision-making process. Notwithstanding, you cannot succeed on stewardship alone – stimuli and the use of power are also essential to financial health. Stimuli surges any financial project through its phases. It spurs you to action and in the development of a successful project helps move it along the path to conclusion. The stimuli resources available to us as controllers influence decisions in the steering of a particular project to its designated, positive outcome. A stimulant is not just an action stemming from a onetime wallet pushed by a family member, friend, business acquaintance, stakeholder, or complete stranger. Economic conditions, opportunities, and adverse situations all serve as fundamental stimuli in the decision process of successful persons. The forces that move us make a great difference in our success. The stimuli that we as Blacks-Latinos-Women receive on a systematic basis definitely has the capacity to advance our chances for success.

If the "put down", as they call it, can be considered "bad" then the lack of stimuli can be considered deadly to Black-Latinos & Women. Generalizations gain no ground for us. The message of this book is this: the responsibility leading to focus and the knowledge belongs to you. Remember: "lack of stimuli can be considered deadly to Blacks, Latinos, & Women."

How often have you seen the "biggest dummy" in charge and successful? It is because they received stimuli in some form along the way. Financial empowerment is a journey and not just a bus stop in the road of life.

Power is executing simple, financial acts to their fullest essence. Power, as of this moment, for each of us may be subdued by stimuli in the forms of family, a friend, a job, social standing, and a lack of education or cash funds. Perhaps we have not yet reached our peak potential. We empathize. Nonetheless, our soul power remains intact for us to use it towards financial success unless we also succumb to negative beliefs which say, "I can't; we can't". Core beliefs about money, success, and the happiness of financial freedom are like a combination number on a bank vault: if we know it, we can open the door.

Story time:

Emmaus is a walk that many Catholics take to further their relationship with Jesus Christ via The Holy Spirit. For Christians, not attuned to the walk, it is a phenomenal life changing event. It is a cleansing of the soul and a renewed path with Jesus the True Friend, Christ and Lord. Truths come during the weekend seminar. One truth that came out is that "I can sugarcoat personal shortcomings by blaming society's injustices". Ouch! But what a relief, when it is no longer, "everyone else has had it easier than me". All people have problems of one type or another. The Power is in overcoming adversity at all reasonable cost. Like Mother Teresa often reminds us: "my ability to do so much came from God." Her earthly opportunity to complete her task came from constantly moving forward against the odds towards a good cause.

When was the last time we got on the bus? Or, are we still at the bus stop, waiting?

"Black Power", a political term of the Sixties, references as a faction in the Civil Rights movement that advocated for self-determination and equality. Though the active reference to "Black Power" is no longer as prominent as it once was, the power of Blacks has definitely evolved over the years. It has undergone a paradigm shift. We can now proudly say that for the first time in United States history, we have a black President in the White House! Today, we need more Black, Latino, & Women Financial Empowerment to have greater voices in individual's minds. The nation and the world, as an infinite business truism, offers the opportunities. The mindset of the go-getter remains the one determining factor in successful personal outcomes, "Cry not, nor weep, for what we may not have fought hard enough for."

Stewardship, stimuli, and power for the majority of citizens regardless of creed, race, color, disability, marital status, or sexual orientation stand as guiding entrances to the greatness of American wealth and financial literacy.

CHAPTER 1.3

PROSPERITY GETS AWAY EVERY DAY I WAIT TO SERVE

The only nice things about financial success seems to be the perks and goodies that come when the cash is in hand. Getting there is another story. The good, profitable ideas seem more difficult to come by in a crowded world of competition. Funding ideas can take a long time in addition to receiving numerous rejections. The hours can be long. The disappointments can be many, only to later find out that it is also, lonely at the top. You say to yourself, is there possibly an easier way to make a living? It is the perfect setting for the enemies of success where procrastination leads to depression deploying a self-feeding habit of negativity.

Psychologists on the whole define procrastination as "an activity that is put to the side". What is the primary cause of procrastination? Is it our preference to do something else? No, it is not the opportunity cost. In actuality it costs opportunities because we know the importance of the activity but still put it aside. One idea creates another idea that leads to a bunch of good ideas, but there is no execution or final result. The time to start or complete something becomes longer than it should. Self-created ideas or imposed responsibility simply does not get acted upon. It matters little about their importance to our future welfare. We just freeze! Certain negative personal results are commonplace, but proper investment activity needs constant reactions to market swings for the short term investor. Entrepreneurs need to update their operations on a timely basis in order to avoid losses and maximize gains. The corporate leaders run around constantly reconfiguring initiatives to produce better returns on investments. They risk losing their checks on the chopping block by the Board of Directors if results are weak. Everyone admittedly procrastinates to some extent. Does it mean that because of a bit of procrastination we are barred from making serious money?

The safeguard against procrastination is to recognize the initial signs in the first place. Rapid, evasive actions prevent us from spinning the wheels into procrastination mode. It protects an individual from feeling depressed at the first sign of business conflict. Growth Action Thinking (GAT) brings to mind the level of consciousness necessary to relieve procrastination pressures. It helps to systematically organize actions in the short-term while keeping a focus on the outcome of simple ideas. Time management serves as a prime weapon against procrastination. A deep personal understanding of one's demons in the surrounding environment and sphere of influence helps us to manage our time better toward Growth Action Thinking Outcomes (GATO).

GATO tramples procrastination at the beginning of the bad habit cycle, conceptualizing a simple idea and its implementation. Three stages support key living money developmental events, guaranteeing personal financial success by laying a planned platform on which to build performance. In the time that it has taken to read these last twelve words, the profits from the money supply have increased enough to either "set us for life" or have us file for bankruptcy. GATO by its nature of predisposed objectives focuses on the appropriate reactions needed to instantaneously address the business conflict at hand. There is no longer any hesitation or anguish in the decision-making process.

Now, a good point to clarify is that investments, entrepreneurship, and corporate leadership represent the identity of the successful financial practitioner. This prosperous figure is just as frightened of failure as the next person with one exception; they understand that guaranteed performance extends from a true relationship in Christ Jesus leading the way. No two portfolios are acted upon by their investors in the same way, even if the stock list and ownership percentile are the same. Each entrepreneur adds his or her style to the same business service. We recognize immediately when the boss at an organization has changed. Our reactions, either positive or negative, are different from one boss to the other doing a similar job. Hence, the fear of not knowing how to format a portfolio, design a business plan, or run a department at work. Even the corporation becomes a mute fear. Mute fears are often best left to silently hang on the Cross because successful people trust in His love. The dreams we share with the Divine manage to find their way to becoming simple, living realities.

"Deep-down motivation has a way of finding your mind and soul after a bit of external soul searching and prayer motivation."(Perez, 2013, 27 Bounce) Growth Action Thinking Outcomes (GATO)

An Expert Tells an Expert Story

"Today I made mocha brownies. What a delight as the house was filled with the rich aroma of chocolate and coffee! I used a box mix and then added my own special touches. "Perfect", said most people as they asked for seconds. I did not make enough for thirds. One hundred percent of my energy and effort produced the tastiest brownies with just enough for two excellent treats per person. Making enough for a third brownie would have meant sacrificing "flavor."

The process of making extra money as an investor relates so well to the allusion of mocha brownies because of the singularly unique characteristics of each activity. Great bakers hold their secrets for each recipe just like the profitable investor understands his or her trade in a particular way. Two investors on a poor day at the markets can either increase or decrease the value of their accounts at different levels. There are no guaranteed outcomes. GATO on the other hand provides gain and controlled loss strategies in relationship to the understanding of the investor. One person might be a know-it-all in tech, consistently reading the latest journals on the subject. She might even attend webinars to keep up to date with the last minute release of Apple products and other fine PC products. Then there's Juanita who cares only about dressing well in the latest fashions. Our two investors naturally understand different markets which equates to reasoning that they will hence, invest based on their respectable knowledge bases. Remember, experts are people who know a lot about one thing and they get paid well for their expertise.

An Expert Tells an Expert Story

ENOUGH! "I always have problems spelling e-n-o-u-g-h. Who knows why I cannot spell such an easy word. Over the years I have attributed it to my nature. The truth is that if I really wanted to I could learn it but I have more important thinking to do, like making sure that this life is not wasted on only focusing on money. Sharing the gifts bestowed upon me with God's people in need must rank high up there as a part of my basic mission ... So, I'll just use spell check."

The truth is that we too often focus our energy on small items that ultimately have simple solutions. Like and understand Apple? Invest in (AAPL) NASDAQ. Like and better understand the clothing market? Invest in Michael Kors Holding Limited (KORS) NYSE. Like bananas, eat and invest in bananas if you understand why there is a possible profit to come from bananas. Get the picture? Every day I wait my money goes away because we tend to procrastinate. Learn what you need to learn. Stop being a chicken and do the right thing for your bank account! By the way, the same goes for, say, the opening of a business or taking over your boss's position. Learn, keep it simple, and do it in the correct spiritual set of mind!

(The companies used are only as examples. No recommendation is being made by the author as to their quality as investment stocks.)

Delaying Your Moneymaking Moment

The mark of a happy human being is to laugh. Therefore, let us laugh at ourselves with realistic critiques from the One-Two Punch Self-test. Answer each question to identify delay and, when applicable, follow the possible solutions to controlling, and dealing with it. It is ultimately an informal, personal assessment about the effects of delay on your wealth and in your life. These indicators can help us to better understand our degree of irreverence toward our bond with money.

The One Two Punch

Do You Delay?

	Punch One: **Recognizing the Presence of "Chicken Fear" Delay**	No	Maybe	Yes
1	My To-Do- List reaches Mars			
2	High-priority money tasks stay undone for 100 years.			
3	Everyone else's emergency comes before mine.			
4	Minor tasks take priority over the bulk of the major money mission.			
5	Do you constantly ask yourself: Is today the right time? Is the market performing at its best?			
6	Can I do investments without some failure?			
7	Did I give thanks on my behalf and prayed to the Lord for others today?			
	Results			
	Punch Two: **Finding the Blame for Delay and Adopting No-Delay Tactics**	No	Maybe	Yes
1	I delay because that is just what I do, OR I delay because I hate the task at hand?			
2	I am disorganized because my peers are also disorganized.			
3	I doubt my spiritual resources in helping me reach for an objective correctly.			
4	I have been told over and over again that I may not have "what it takes" to do it.			
5	Society wants me to fail.			
	Results			

Intentional blank page for reader's notes:

If you answered "yes" to 4 or more questions for the 1-2 Punch Self-test you may find the tips below helpful in rectifying the presence of Delay in your financial life.

Punch One – Recognizing the Presence of Delay

The understanding of delay, or outright procrastination, depends on us, the task at hand, and a few relevant environmental factors. Clear recognition of which factors play the greater role becomes our secret to unfolding our lack of action. GATO helps us realize that good intentions are powerful! GAT helps us create a greater shift toward natural and spiritual organization. We may be afraid! But if we're organized, we feel less overwhelmed by the task.

Everyone senses fear of sustained accomplishment at any specific moment. This spontaneous fear can lead to the doubt of our own skills or resources in accomplishing a goal. Hence, we seek comfort in doing tasks which appear simple enough to enhance the proof of completion.

Do we, then maybe fear success even more than failure? Is failure so friendly to us that we welcome it with open arms? Why does such a small amount of the population deal in successful abundance with personal finances? For example, do you think that success will lead you to being swamped with more requests to do several tasks you dislike? Or that you'll be pushed to take on responsibilities that you feel are beyond you? All in all, delaying to increase personal wealth boils down to just being a dumb chicken. If helpful, go see a psychologist with a high hourly professional fee to prove whether the above statement is true. The lack of knowledge regarding your delay will only lead to more "procrastination".

Punch Two – Finding the Blame for Our Delay

Causes of delay may stem from social forces that continuously associate modern heroes to materialistic success stories. A rather better comparison is one in which the imperfect humans just managed to do well for themselves. Such comparisons may thrust us into a citadel of perfection, where we are forced to seek nothing other than perfect control to feel successful. To be perfect in outcomes, you can hence, mistakenly believe that all resources and personal abilities must be at 100% efficiency to reach success. The truth is that trying to become perfect or nothing else all the time leads to never creating a final product. The time to accomplish most things is, then, normally flanked by a lack of resources or personal ability. Tenacity the skill of relentlessly pushing forward, coupled with a well-developed decision-making habit is overrun due to an imagined lack of resources or ability.

Unfortunately, the need for more money in our modern world is not going to go away. Inflation, increased personal use of costly technology, desires for upscale lifestyles, the need for higher education, and the general complexities of modern life have become routine to human existence. Regardless of how money intertwines in our lives, we can grow into a better relationship with personal finances. It is simple. Make finances work for you, not the other way around.

Implement No-Delay Tactics

I personally eat cheese, chocolate, strawberries and drink Champagne to celebrate the great moments in my life. It is a habit that I have practiced for many years and that has evolved to become a deeply ingrained, characteristic behavior. Other people practice similar behaviors to celebrate equally superior moments in their lives. What do you do? A habit may or may not be a bad one but it is the changing or elimination of a habit that causes difficulty for most of us. We dream of 24 hour solutions, as if changing an ingrained habit is the same as a dental extraction in getting rid of a tooth ache, when in fact it is more like by-pass surgery. We wish procrastination was easy to get out of our lives. Overall, it's a strong notion to understand that delay won't just be broken overnight. It won't be a onetime stopping of procrastination. The fight against procrastination is an indefinite one.

One major problem with managing money and finances is the time sensitivity of fiscal matters. The appropriate action taken at the precise time of possible maximum gain will produce unimaginable profits. Sitting on the decision to take the action at the right time, may very well cause you to lose your shirt. Hence, the self-control of delay in financial actions will help to make you affluent. What can we do to safeguard against delay from keeping away affluence?

Tactics:
- Create a *personal rewards system* to commemorate finished tasks and milestones.
- Include an element of peer pressure by asking a friend to push you a little when you fall behind target performance.
- *Identify* distasteful tasks but place emphasis on the enjoyable parts of them.
- *Quantify* the consequences of NOT doing a task.
- Bring the *To-Do List* down from Mars into a realistic, daily work plan.
- Organize tasks to be done into an *Urgent, Important, When Possible Matrix* system of your own. Keep it simple.
- Master the art of *project planning* with precise schedules and a time line.
- Break a larger task into a smaller task: change wanting to "make the million" into making the first thousand, and continue in one thousand intervals until you hit your larger goal.
- If you do not like the task of, say, fundamental analysis hurry up and finish it anyway.
- Consider risk a "friend". Get to know it so you can deal with it in a profitable partnership.
- Think to yourself: *I am no stupid chicken so I must train for investing, opening that new business, or becoming a senior VP.*
- Get that resume ready. Apply now for that administrative position.
- Give thanks for what you have now. See how you can better serve humanity as a consequence of reaching your next prosperity level.

Closing thoughts and my personal experiences on Procrastination and Delay:

Once, a millionaire friend did not lend me $75,000 to buy a piece of land worth $125,000, which was a low estimate, because she said that I "took too long" to make a decision. Three weeks later I came across another deal for $300,000 and she bankrolled it. It took two days to complete, due diligence and make my decision, that it was a possible good deal. A decision has to be made if we are to succeed. Possible failure is just another part of the game much like the recreational enjoyment of the ocean. Do not fear it, respect it. Florida has palms that perfectly meet their environmental surroundings due to their extreme flexibility. During hurricanes, palms tend to survive over other strong harder non-flex trees due to this flexible nature. Let nothing overwhelm you, just change the routine to accommodate personal style for getting things finished on time.

All in all, these time honored suggestions may help stimulate you to keep moving toward your financial goals, and guard against the damaging effects that are delay and procrastination. I must confess that my own routine prayers include, a request for me not to procrastinate, and complete my God-given opportunities while here on earth.

2
REVELATIONS OF AFFLUENCE

Holistic Rewards After A New "Personal Baseline"

CHAPTER 2.1

SHOULD WE LET LOSERS HELP US FAIL?

It's a beautiful Saturday mid-afternoon: sunny, the temperature in the lower seventies, a perfect time to escape the family and the world by shopping at Wal-Mart. All I needed was a quart of boat motor oil, some salty snacks, and the fixings required to mix a quality margarita for a planned boat trip out in the bay Sunday after Church. Boom! A loser sighting! As it turned out, it was a loser encounter by one of the clerks at the store that caught my attention. She had been married to a loser at age 24. Now, at age 40, she was working like a fool for minimum wage, attending school again, and raising a 16 year old boy all on her own. At the moment, she is emptying a bushel of limes to restock the produce shelf. Yes, fresh lime juice is what I like for the perfect margarita. The woman recognized me from some marketing campaign material that a friend had given her about one of my GAT workshops.

We tend to find lovers and losers during times of promise in our lives. At age 24, touched by the gift of attractiveness that comes to us all during the early years of life, Alison found a guy that smelled and sounded charming. We fall in love in our twenties as part of natures' guarantee for the next human generation. It is also a fertile time in life where we sow our financial environments in hopes of harvesting stable economic futures. If we meet the God-loving person that is meant to complement our nature, we tend to move on through life in happiness. If we meet a person emotionally mature enough to understand the deep need for education, especially for us both then we tend to move on through life in a mode that is satisfying financially. The trick is more than luck. The trick is to position ourselves in a time and place where it is easy to find the right soul mate. It might come as a type of aphrodisiac in that someone compliments our hearts, prospers the pocketbook, or honors individualistic persona. But most of all, one should look for these humanly actions from a consciously growing belief in God. Only then should we have fun letting those sweet words charm our pants off.

Alison did what many young people do. She fell in love, gave up her studies, got together with the guy, and had a baby boy. Now, her 16-year-old child has been both a blessing and a pain to raise on her own. What simple ideas can she now possibly manipulate into her life to make up for lost time? My sister, Maya, has a saying: "The unwise young waste time, the elderly want it back, and the wise middle-aged try to repair its passing." What Maya never says, however, is that we can get lost time back. The value of time refines our lives as we shower in its present, gracious glory. It matters not whether times are good or bad; but rather our current time runs parallel with the current moment. Alison is searching for an economic answer that is impossible to find without God. She, like most of us, at some point just wants time back.

Any present success in my life has its limits based on the level of control others try to take over it. The action of small changes in thinking represents the right path to fresher more significant goals. If personal betterment moves from a distant dream to real achievement then promises to oneself are found in those actions which helps us to grow to the next level of successful and happier living. To acquire a change agent to lead us, we can find moments of reflection which lead to personal knowledge and advanced inspiration. A simple look to the past can reveal certain change agents in our lives. It can be a teacher, a parent, God through scripture, a friend, a mentor, or even an isolated action from a stranger at a gas station. The inspirations or negative effects upon us from other people are universal and inescapable. A simple story of my personal remembrance may help you to see the concept more clearly.

My dad, after two years of serious cancer treatments, is ready to meet the Lord. As a very powerful and caring figure in my life, he leaves his love and words of moral support as a memory. How do I cope? Do I transgress the beliefs and common core lifestyle of my family or accept a completely new way of life? Do I take lessons from his death concerning my upbringing? Or do I unquestionably accept the new norms of gaining wealth which may include questionable ethics and general mistrust of financial institutions or business partners?

Simple evaluation of personal values is a common denominator in valuing the influences of newcomers into our lives. While newcomers allow us to expand thinking and possibly gain more opportunities, personal, integral knowledge also supports our decision-making process. It allows us to proceed without fear to follow our hearts. The simple idea of internet communication as an example helps us to instantly assert the human nature to desire good news. The inventors of social media use the current setup of the internet and e-mail system to create their own social media world. If the success of the internet is a mixture of old fundamental human nature and new technological resources, we can use its influence either for good or bad personal fiscal outcomes. The pending quest now develops into a formulation through quick analysis and due diligence of ideas to gain affluence in a form that stays true to our hearts: benefits for our pocketbook plus responsible, social, spiritual stewardship. What a great moment to sing songs like "All You Need Is Love", "Happy", "Beer With Jesus", or whatever other personal, positive lyrics that inspire us at the moment.

Violating the simple, natural rule of having an intended personal movement will keep us from moving forward until unintended interruptions cause it to happen. The first incident may be influenced by acquaintances of unscrupulous professionals. The second follows changes in the business environment, a phenomenon that is a natural occurrence to all business endeavors. Finally, the third determinant of how high we succeed is based on ones lack of continuous growth derived as a product of peer interchange and individual exploration of the business area. Yes, the road can turn into a lonely highway. It sounds like once we are in motion, staying in motion takes life-long effort for substantial life-long returns. This is where God-given wisdom to select business associations remains a simple guarantee for success. If we have the wisdom to hang with the right crowd then we will do just fine.

Please follow this simple idea. Yesterday morning, Juanita's scale showed a loss of one and three-quarter pounds. Congrats, girl! Juanita's new date then invites her to a fancy, romantic, Caribbean eatery by the glistening moon lit coast. Her date takes liberties to impress by ordering for them both while she washes her hands in the luxurious restroom. The waiters begin to bring servings of sweet rum mojitos, warm Cuban bread smothered with garlic butter, fried plantain chips, jumbo shrimp cocktails, baskets of conch fritters, and sweet potato bacon soup followed by rounds of mojitos and a bottle of Dom Perignon champagne. The main course: medallions of fillet mignon in creamy coconut cilantro sauce side mounted with two king size lobster tails flaming in cognac. After dinner, mild, sweet zinfandel wine while the crowning desert fit for royalty arrives: chocolate dipped jumbo strawberries atop warm banana mango walnut cake and creamy vanilla ice cream drizzled with a cream Kahlua chocolate topping. The dinner ends with a sip of Sambuca infused with coffee beans as they view the moon's reflection on the sea. Hah! Don't we all need a date with this kind of wallet power!

Okay, take a break… Back to reality. The next morning, Juanita has a gain of 2 pounds… We know what caloric burning activities she could have done the rest of the night... but she didn't! She has a goal despite influences that attempt to undermine her determination. Juanita is focused on her losses. She follows the evening with a three mile morning walk which reactivates her metabolism in the right direction.

No one successful investor, upcoming corporate leader, or business owner can survive or succeed in today's fast-paced business environment without mentors who support and challenge them in the proper spirit of success.

CHAPTER 2.2

THE MOST EFFECTIVE, LOVING MONEY FUND MANAGER

Two Thirty Four and Three Little Lines

Poem by Theo Smith

The first step is difficult to take morning after morning as we awake.
Through the same personal shame another day to face.
The overweight tower of personal junk piles high crushing our pride.

"Have I turned my eyes inward to face my river of sins? Hopefully everyone does once in a while."

Our lives divided from the joy of freedoms versus sparring against the heavy responsibilities of living.
We are seemingly conquered by the moments in time provided for existence.
Children play for only the moments that their parents say it is okay.
Young workers must toil until the boss says "no more today", until

the next incoming shift's moment.
The moment for love hits our time just to feel restricted by society's ties.
I complain trying to go in some other, unlimited way.

"Have I turned my eyes inward to face my river of sins? Hopefully everyone will once in a while."

The bride and new husband are sworn in a moment to look no other way.
The baby, bill collectors, a beer or a joint are more frequent moments than a satisfying job we can hold.
Our sky seems gray on sunny days.

"Have I turned my head to face my river of sins? Hopefully everyone has once in a while."

Our responsibilities pain our way each day.
Our mounting tower is a pile of personal junk that must be shared in order to bare.
Our bad habits sooner or later pain the ones we love.
We, I must find a way....

"Have I turned my head to face my river of sins? Hopefully I still can once in a while."

Our diminishing pile of personal junk becomes possible to bare through prayer.

And I turn my eyes upward to share my river of sins every once in a while in faith that HE cares. For Christ bowed his head to face our river of sins. Hopefully everyone once in a while remembers.

The destiny of prosperity is self-built as we naturally fulfill God's eternal love for us. The pit of despair and complaining concerning natural material desires and the lack of economic resources can be changed for the better. God loves His people! He sent His Son, Jesus, to save us! He enlightens us through the Holy Spirit! And, filled with grace, the Blessed Mother, Mary, to comfort us! What better showing of love do we need to realize that He is on our side? Are we on His side? It takes a team to succeed in the game of life. Personal business management is an integral part of financial life but in this modern world it can overcome life altogether. MAT 23:1-7 speaks to the awesome love of our Lord and Christ's message of love for us.

Motivated to Succeed

Personal success is often connected to destructive arrogance, frustration, and loneliness. Meanwhile the attainment of true personal success reflects so much more than just the capture of material possessions or the ability to feel accomplished. True personal triumph need not keep us from finding love.

> GAT's relation to its practitioners remains an ultimate ongoing discussion of mutual dedication to achievement in life. We suggest the right ideas, in the right disposition, while your desire to make a change in life is at its highest need. It's about opening the doors and inviting your personal victory with supportive motivation.
>
> GATAS (Growth Action Thinking Advantage Strategies) makes something that seems unattainable easy to possess. Try an idea following participation in a GAT group and you will notice a difference in your confidence level.

From your first interactions you will already realize how to accomplish what you need to prosper. That is personal success!

Every idea we've ever explored is there to increase true personal growth. The opportunity to avoid the wrong approach is present. We can now reconsider destructive arrogance and frustration: they are no longer part of our purpose because of the supreme divinity in our successful lives.

A simpler, more useful, more enjoyable, more powerful fruitful life experience is the reward for *GAT* members.

Experience It for Yourself

Go look at the all-new discussions in life achievement. *Love God in Others!*

Transforming From a Dull Light Bulb to an LED

The scriptures correlating the Fifth Sunday for the Roman Catholic calendar on February 9th, 2014 focused on our true light as a reflection of the quality of servitude each of us provide as witnesses of Christian love. In service inherent to our soul, we provide the most spiritually guided benefits to society. We also gain the closest alignment with spiritual, human perfection. Dedicated service to our true nature places our life's work one more step on the road to salvation. The reading sequence emphasizing the living God's purpose for our life is contained in *[Isaiah 58:7-10; Psalm 112; 1 Corinthians 2:`1-5; and Matthew 5:13-16]*. These scriptural, eye opening clarifications support the simple idea that we are not foolish or extreme for shooting for our dreams.

In contrast, following everyone else to attain the superficial glitters of success is contrary to God-given zests embodied to us with trustworthy fidelity. If we do not take the time, effort, and commitment to explore and execute God's-given talents as the manifestations of His love in our lives then we become lifeless, burnt out light bulbs. The brightness that may be enjoyed by others is gone.

Success in all aspects of life, especially financially, demands us to take a risk in conjunction with a leap of faith. We live the best following our good heart. The All Mighty empowers our lives to react to the needs of others. Our nature is meant to be that of a provider. However, in order to properly provide, we must pursue activities which create sufficient revenue for the care of the Church, others, and ourselves. Have no fear. You are not alone!

The "Life Kicks" That Bring Us Down and Pull Us Back Up

THE LOSS OF LOVE OR MONEY, BY ANY MEANS, HURTS US IN MANY WAYS. The start of this book gives consideration to a simple idea merging proper knowledge of financial terms with the investor's growing ability towards appreciation of economic opportunities. It is paramount for successful business financiers. We are ready for a business journey traveling from point A to point B mapped out as if on a bus route towards financial freedom. Now, the question remains; who are the people we can trust on our journey?

Mentors at this juncture in life may cause monumental anguish to our minds, bodies, and souls. Their views on the creation of wealth may clash with 21st Century opportunities to make the cash. A variety of methods are available for people to apply their style to the process of making money. All styles are worthy of equal recognition:
    1.   Conceding the practitioner style of the investor;
    2.   Applauding the pioneering spirit of the entrepreneur;
    3.   We also support the aspiring nature of the corporate leader.
All three styles of developing wealth require savvy individual effort and some type of support team to make the endeavor work. Mentors

at this juncture may again try to instill a questionable mindset of caution based on the irreverence associated with being prosperous. Why do we think that money is considered "the root of all evil" as well as the cure for most needs?

The general belief is that money makes people evil. God and money in the same sentence are often paired as opposites. But this is far from the truth. A realistic debate remains an important focus here in terms of a strong relationship between our strength of faith in God and the ability to become prosperous. God-devoted people do attain wealth. People of faith do find ways to make money that are both humanistic and positive. They use their capital investments for the good of others without restraint of their Christian fundamentals. (We shall explore more of this concept in section 2.3.)

We are not to cheat. We are not to lie. We are not to honor money or its power. Yes, we recognize the worldly necessity for it. So, as a result, we use wealth appropriately to meet the needs of the Church, the needy community, and ourselves. This Faith position in the distribution of wealth creates a karma which returns goodness that is to be shared in our lives. We are to do unto others as we would like them to do unto us. We are to also give and to never expect receiving anything back.

The limited time we have to do well can be enhanced by our relationship with the most effective, loving money fund manager. Money management, portfolio management, or the creation of personal wealth represents just another stewardship opportunity. God, in his omnipotence, provides the stewardship opportunity. It is our responsibility to learn well, grow, and distribute the fruits.

CHAPTER 2.3

THE GOODNESS OF MONEY

On Earth, we often grapple with our responsibility to flower as children of God. We often go through life as if no GPS has been given to us. The powers to help the churches, the oppressed, and the needy are fine talents that have already been given to us. Investment trading, offering dignified places for others to live, honorably practicing a profession or career, and opening businesses are just some of the fine earthly affairs we can go about.

We may view others' ways of acting towards the material and the spiritual as isolated from one another but the birthright is actually already in our hearts. This acknowledgement shapes and supports us as true children of God, uniting the material and the spiritual to relate to one another. Depending on which way we lean, we may then subconsciously or deliberately have mindsets for action that slow us down and even stop us from becoming everything that is meant for us.

Wickedness is imparted when we idolize manna only for its worldly images. We have the free choice of practicing the power of capitalist materialism in humble ways that help our fellow sisters and brothers. When was the last time you stopped your money-making rush to enjoy the disappearance of the stars and the moon into the glorious glaze of the morning sun? When did you last put your hand up to the sky and breathe in the fresh air that surrounds you? When was the last time in that early evening drive on a crowded highway did you realize that billions of people on earth do not enjoy our fancy rides? Did you pray last night to thank God for all that you had during the day's labor?

The Catholics, like other Christian believers, pray, among other things, for prosperity. Part of the Catholic Mass includes a ceremonial moment when the congregation says the "Prayer of The Faithful", which is a number of alms and petitions. It is then followed by proverbs said by a priest who then leads the congregation into the Stewardship prayer.

The December 1st, 2013 reader's sheet where I got this prayer at Mother of Our Redeemer Church reads as follow: (It is OK to pray)

> "Oh, God. Our loving Creator and Giver of all good gifts / bless our parish / strengthen our faith / and grant us the spirit of Christian Stewardship / so that we may give generously of our time / talent and treasure / to the spreading of Your Kingdom here at .../ and throughout the world. We ask this through Christ, our Lord. Amen."

Now tell yourself that money is bad! It is about what we do to people in the process of getting it. It is how we get it that makes it questionable. It is whether we become greedy when we have it. It is whether our relationship with money has been affecting our positive relationship with God. We are to love God above all. Some people start to love money above all. Get your relationships allied with God. Stop working for just money as the sole purpose for living. Money is just a product of an honest day's labor, investments, or trading activities. These three resources are creations of God for His beloved children to manage, just like everything else on earth. A fear of not having money is irrelevant for a child of God maintaining a good relationship with the Father.

Taking a deep point of individual meditation often helps align prosperity with greater happiness. Nevertheless, many people tend to get caught up in a quasi-planned rat race. Rather than going with positive, personal opinions we forget the true reasons for life's energy. We instead transgress by valuing ideas from the media, propaganda houses, wacky partners, and enslaving, oppressive, social norms.

The chart below follows interpretations of archaic thinking that meets some of our current, economic circumstances:

Personal Virtue	Simple, Modern Interpretation 1 = archaic thinking 2 = modern interpretation	Find it in the Scriptures
Morality	1. "Money is not for hiring dancing harlots and paying for booze, drugs or other excessive vices. It is also not a collectable item to gather dust." Wealth does not bring honor, nor true prosperity. 2. Good, plentiful monetary gifts come from making money through clean, honorable, respectful sources. We are to bring goodness to others by our quality service, generosity, and sharing. It is the only way to gather the true treasures of an eternal life.	Luke 15:11-19 Parable of the Lost Son Ephesians 4:19 Immoral gluttony James 4:17 Not doing good work 1Timothy 6:18 Joy of good work
Faith	1. "You think you make your own money from your own sweat? When was the last time you woke up without God giving you the power to breathe or sweat?" 2. We should not worry ourselves with getting monetary advantage on our own. God will provide. The faith to believe in Him is all we need. Have faith in what He set us out to accomplish during our short stay on earth. He has given us personal abilities for the production, gathering, and managed distribution of His financial resources. Prosperity is acting like His stewards in service.	James 4: 13 Presumptions John 9:4 Grab His opportunity 3 John 2-4 Wealth, health from spiritual vitality

Responsibility	1. Give unto Cesar as they did in the Old Testament. Be thankful we can grumble about paying high taxes every April 15th.	1 Corinthians 16:2 Stewardship
	2. The House of Prayer costs money to operate. Be thankful for God's gift by making sizeable donations and the giving of stewardship, time, and talent. Florida Power & Light, for example, does not give free electricity to churches. We, the parishioners, tend to want air conditioning in a beautiful, comfortable church without leaky roofs. Clergy personnel also have to be available during extended hours to meet increasing needs as a result of our desire for constant, community activity. Donations serve to benefit all. Prosperity enters our lives from giving generously.	

Remember: money, in itself, is not bad! It can actually be the lock or key on Heaven's door. We may just want to develop archaic thinking into simple, modern interpretations that meet current and future economic circumstances. I understand that these last few paragraphs of reading have been so intense that your mind might feel sweaty. Therefore, let's go easy for now but continue to fortify our brains with financial thinking as it relates to <u>morality, faith, and responsibility</u>.

Yes, we also need to consider the exasperation of seemingly working "for nothing". Nonetheless we need to take this moment to consider the luminous effect of being alive in a mindset that nurtures work that is appreciated by God. Work answers the needs of our fellow human beings in addition to material desire.

3

A JOYFUL PROSPEROUS LIFE

Receive The Empowerment of Prosperity

CHAPTER 3.1

GAT: THE THREE PHASES TO EMPOWERED PROSPERITY

The new USA economy demands a sense of personal urgency for self-finance management to be effective enough for long-term success. Many people maintain continuous dialogue about personal growth directed by focused actions. They want to reach a next level of success as part of a happier life. Some of us seek greater financial security and independence. Others aspire to climb the corporate mountain while the maverick group desires the growth of a personal business venture. Living Money Bound participants can make one of their most significant personal gains and family contributions through the use of the simple thinking process of **Growth Action Thinking (GAT)** by following three phases.

GAT is a life planning, decision-making, and goal reaching tool that helps us change the outcome of problems overwhelming our current lives by attempting to master our personal futures for the better. GAT produces flexible and adaptable answers rather than fixes outdated conclusions that fail during stormy times. GAT defines where we as individuals **desire to go! GAT helps us reflect** about the best possible decisions. GAT clearly defines, lists, and helps pledge the resources to reach our goals. It is not only financial planning but a planning in personal, holistic strategy.

The difficulties, opportunities, aspirations and joys of daily living are the vital ingredients for exploration in constant personal growth. The well-designed GAT process binds worthy simple ideas with the use of quality time and resources. The focus is the basis of our needs, desires, and roots in financial problems. The conclusion is a set of applicable holistic solutions that resolve individual challenges long-term. A style of Living Money Bound encourages support and solutions via an in-depth process over a number of months via the three phases as follows:

> GAT offers a one day gathering. It is a memorable, fun, and growth experience. We meet to vent out our money frustrations. Yes, someone actually listens! We meet to find solutions. We receive mentoring and other resources which elevate our financial lives to the next level. Living Money Bound readers who also attend a GAT seminar as participant practice with their simple ideas, and gain an exclusive collection of life's financial business knowledge.

PHASE ONE [Living Overview]

- **Engage in meaningful conversation** with Mentor Members, family, business partners, and current or future creditors to hear and evaluate needs, wants, and aspirations.
- **Complete "personal situation probes"** to isolate personal habits as financial/social trends in reference to dynamic forces in the economy.
- **Recognize competitive challenges** with potential for greater financial sustainability through teamwork.
- **Reflect on spiritual** and family relationships.

PHASE TWO [Money Factors]

- **Briefly explore new financial** models to see what advantages they could bring for you.
- **Examine values, priorities**, and options for personal development.
- **Analyze complete living costs**; develop budget objectives and select methods for money resources expansion.
- **Assess the valuable strengths of resources**, support services, and programs with a focus on personal requirements to make them more substantial for personal goal attainment.

PHASE THREE [Bound to Future Growth]

- **Affirm** with Growth Action Thinking (GAT) the personal mission to decide long-term goals that set the stage for simple short-term actions.
- **Empower** with simple actions the most inspiring personal vision to energize life-long change.
- **Acknowledge the presence of spiritual** and family relationships as a factor in the financial decision.
- **Develop helpful indicators** to monitor progress, achievements and decide how to use the updated method to guide continuous Growth Action Thinking.

Personal actions such as GAT share the platform with established inspirational methods of obtaining personal success. The GAT growth, however, seems to come from dual zones of quality results and good personal feelings.

GATAS©

(Growth Action Thinking Advantage Strategy)

Life planning tools help any sensible person who attempts to master a future full of success. Planning for abundance and realization of personal ideas requires tangible forms of gathering thoughts for a process of development, exploration, selection, implementation, and review in the form of reflection. **GATAS©** specifically guides the user to bring into being flexible, plausible solutions adaptable to a variety of lane changes on the highway to success. All actions take place without missing the original destination. It is similar to driving a vehicle using GPS on unfamiliar, busy, fast moving roads. That little voice that prompts you to turn at the right moment helps. Let **GATAS©** help you in the same way! Good solid planning naturally increases our confidence that each decision will be good for us. The following is a series of exercises in **GATAS©**

GATAS© Soul Search	My True Thoughts In Raw Form			
Idea ☼	Problem ☼	Opportunity ☼	Desire ☼	Decision ☼
Instruction 1: Select one ☼ → personal issue to empower with GAT.				
Instruction 2: I need to write down my raw feelings. *This is not school! It is real life. No one else is going to read these words unless I allow them to. I can forget about spelling and grammar. I must be brutally honest, clear and to the point. This simple action is the foundation for any personal growth.*				
Instruction 3: Take Action. Complete each of the boxes below by answering the simple "WHAT".				

"WHAT" I already know: ☼:_____	"WHAT" I need to find out to move forward:	"WHAT" might I do with this newly found information:

Now that I got out of my mind some real honest thoughts about ☼ _____, the next step is to state issues in a way (if needed) that can be shared with others.

GATAS© Development	Personal Issue I Desire to Apply to Practicing GAT		
	End my financial frustrations ☼	Satisfy urges to climb for better job ☼	Finally open my business ☼
Select one Arena ☼ →			
Instruction 4:	"WHY" do I choose this arena to empower my life using GAT?		
Now we have empowered the true emotional awareness related to personal issues.			
Select a success arena in which to manifest your excellence using simple ideas.	"WHY" not choose some different goal to raise my life's present position?		
Answer the simple "WHY"? It is a growth action thinking process which clarifies where we are as a person now! We also find out where our journey of affluence will take us.	"WHY" do I revolt against my position in which I currently exist?		

I have identified a personal issue which needs a new direction from me. I believe that _____ serves as a good focus arena for me to work intelligently in a growing demonstration of success.

**Intentional blank page for reader's notes:
[For GATAS© Soul Search and Development]**

The next step is to expand the issue in a way that, if need be, an immediate opportunity can be quickly explored because we already placed it on our list for consideration.

GATAS© Exploration	Time to Explore Possibilities	
Instruction 5: **Now that we have motioned toward a different, hopefully higher, better, easier, happier, or more affluent life, do two simple growth actions.** The first one is to list all actions which anyone, including me, might do to find an answer to my personal issue. The second thing is to not judge them in any way, nor change the way that I originally thought of it.	Insert any and all things for consideration which anyone might do.	Insert any and all things for consideration which I might do.
Instruction 6: **Keeping in mind what I said during questions one through four, it is time for another simple action.**	Insert selected things for consideration from the top list which anyone might do.	Insert selected things and rate for consideration which I might do.

List all suggestions from the top lists which I like more.		

Instruction 7:
 	
Research time... Anything for consideration from either list which I move to the next decision making process must first receive what lawyers and accountants call "due diligence".
 	
    It is just to find out the truth of what I am about to get into.
 	
    If I cannot handle that truth, the selected thing in question does not move on to the next level. Simple!
	Use the back of this paper or a different sheet of paper to complete the research. Use multiple resources.	

Without panic, hard work, or people meddling in our lives [unless I prefer to be public], simple actions are moving me to a true, personal decision of success. Undertaking the process itself creates a feeling of accomplishment.

**Intentional blank page for reader's notes:
[For GATAS© Exploration]**

The next step leads to a quality decision.

GATAS© Selection	Simple Selection Process			
Instruction 8: **It is time for a strategic tool which provides equality for my different ideas before I formulate an opinion.** I will use a Ṭ for listing what I view as a positive or negative for me. *I must love myself and trust my feelings. Simply using my mind as far as I can push myself.* It must be done without fear or "complejos". [shame]	Use the back of this paper, different sheets, or a computer to complete the **Ṭ's.** Here is a sample.			
	GATAS© Selection Ṭ	List or Describe One Simple Idea:		
	Ṭ Good Things	Ṭ Bad Things	Possible Outcomes	
Instruction 9: **Pick based on GATO (Growth Action Thinking Outcome) what outcome suits me best.**	Action for Implementation		Expected Outcomes from this simple action	

Instruction 10: **Make sure that I support the action with spiritual resources to guarantee success.** Notes: **Relate a spiritual and personal place during every action.**	List and describe all steps which I must take to reach success. Do the same for any needed resource. DO NOT STOP DOING THESE SIMPLE ACTIONS UNTIL I REACH SUCCESS FOR THIS PARTICULAR GOAL.	
	STEPS:	RESOURCES:

The correct personal simple action to activate affluence with happiness in my life is now underway.

THE NEXT STEP ONLY REQUIRES CONSTANT MONITORING OF THE CONSEQUENCES FORMING IN OUR LIVES.

"I WILL CONTINUE TO FOCUS ON A POSITIVE, HAPPY ABUNDANCE DURING DAILY LIVING."

"I WILL SERVE PEOPLE IN NEED AS A PATH TO MY PROSPERITY"

- **Gathering my thoughts**
- **Process development**
- **Exploration**
- **Selection**
- **Review in the form of revelation**

Growth Action Thinking defines where we as individuals **desire to go! GAT helps us reflect** about the best possible decisions. Again, Growth Action Thinking clearly defines, lists, and then helps pledge the resources to reach our goals. It is not only financial but a great personal strategy.

CHAPTER 3.2

MONEY WORKING FOR YOU
24 HOURS A DAY

Everyone would like to know direct answers on how to make extra money by capitalizing in their economic opportunities. Bernice, as we shall call her, was relaxing in a rocking chair when I arrived to collect the rent. She was twenty-nine years old, well robed in a Versace beach dress, and spending the winter season at a waterfront studio I owned by South Beach. It was mid-afternoon and warm, a time when most adults were laboring at their forty hour jobs. She appeared to have always been very thin and sickly-looking but she had a natural, soft beauty about her face. Her smile was usually harmonious and her eyes were worry-free, as if at peace with God and herself. She had no husband, no children, and no first line relatives to my knowledge except for a male friend with whom she migrated from a nearby Caribbean island three years earlier.

After Bernice's wet arrival to the shores of Florida, she received the standard United States financial aid package given to qualifying immigrants. Refugee aid included medical care, medicines, housing assistance, food stamps, English classes, and job training seminars for a limited time. She took advantage of it all. The English classes were very difficult but eventually resulted in her speaking and reading the new language with proficiency. The government's expenditure on job training seminars turned out to be a good use of taxpayer money. Together with the English classes, she decided to take a seminar series about becoming a stock broker. Bernice understandably failed because of the language barrier. She took away what she could: a different approach to handling money. There WAS ANOTHER WAY other than laboring for some unbearable employer for little pay. With learning simple GAT ideas, and with a focus on investing, she can increase her level to make money!

Now, here comes the practical side to Bernice's following of GAT: LIVING MONEY BOUND IS ABOUT MOTIVATING OURSELVES TO BOUNCE INTO FINANCIAL STABILITY WHICH WILL KEEP OUR LIFE IN PROSPERITY. It is about moving, or being *money* bound, towards financial freedom. In contrast, it also refers to the opposite in how having a low paying job and an excess of bills can bind you. Formal studies will further your understanding of money to enter the world of investments. Regardless of whether there are clues, or even a starting point, Bernice shows that it takes individual responsibility to be prosperity bound.

People who feel a need for others to manage their personal finances use brokers. There is nothing wrong with brokers. But remember: if both of your wallets fall into a river, which wallet will be recovered first? Now, I don't want to offend any of my professional friends but none of them manage my money. The few brokers that I have used in the past considered me a client who paid their livelihoods. I made sure they had proven expertise, diligence, and transparency interweaved into their souls. Therefore, they acted and performed as the contracted, dispensable, transferable professionals that they were. Do we let dishonest, incompetent fools squander our money? No! We are the sole responsible party in dealing with our money matters (talents). God provides the opportunities, we expand them as honor to Him, in service to others, and livelihood for ourselves.

If you do decide to use a broker, take the time to answer a few relevant questions:

Broker Questions	Fill-in Simple Idea Answer
What data do brokers use to base their recommendations?	
Do you receive clear and sound explanations?	
How much of my capital goes to fees and unneeded expenses?	
How much is my return on the investment impacted?	
Am I offered a wide range of opportunities or just precise investment products?	
How do I understand the progress of my financial goals?	
Do they describe the set benchmarks advised to me from the use of tracking tools?	
Does my broker discuss the risks in my investment portfolio?	
Do I feel completely comfortable discussing personal situations with the broker?	
Do I hire a team of professionals or just one person?	
Which is my preference: for the broker to be actively involved in my investment strategy or for the broker to just sit by the sidelines as another resource?	
Is the level of professional attention questionable?	

We go to the doctor to tell them how lousy we feel. The doctor examines the area in poor health and writes a few medical terms in the long yellow page of our medical chart. We hear the ailment in complicated, fancy medical terms and get a prescription. Did you understand what the doctor said? No, not all of it. Should you go buy the prescription and follow his directions? Yes, because it most likely will work. The doctor studied too long, too much, and is up to date on medical stuff that I know can save my life. I do what they tell me all the time. Besides, a doctor's fundamental nature is one of care for mankind rather than selling over the quota, making a commission, and getting a bonus. Thus, a broker is not a doctor.

Hit the floor; most financial pros are about to throw this book up in the air or across the room! How dare I even think that doctors are more compassionate than financial staffers selling money-making products and services! All in all, I am not questioning integrity here but I am saying that doctors are usually there to help us out. Case in point: the recent fiascos at Wall Street and the self-serving mortgage default industry.

Any final, financial decisions are solely in your power as the investor. Oh yes, I called us INVESTORS! Financial experts are fine to have as consultants for the fundamental learnings, specific investigations, and for the processes of decision-making. Personal, financial health may well be reached by most individuals if they just try to learn about their money.

Important Definitions to Consider

We need to understand money in simpler terms. In fact, one simple idea can make us a lot of money: buy low and sell a bit higher. A second thing to remember: look at current world news and events. Decide outcomes based on news information. Enter and exit the market as circumstances change making sure to always look out for your favor. And most important of all, <u>if you do not get informed</u> and act, YOU WILL LOSE YOUR MONEY!

A personal understanding of money language is very important. The investment industry loves to complicate simple trade ideas. They turn them into monsters that only Wall Street brokerages can resolve by charging another unnecessary fee. *"Fiat Money"* is one definition we need to understand to make money in buying and selling currency.

Fiat Money

Understand It As:
Physical reserves of gold or silver not used as <u>intrinsic value</u> by countries in assessing their money. On pure faith, the value is declared legal by governments as an economic standing in gross national production, exports, imports, tourism, national debt and civil stability. The perception of global trading mechanisms also influence value.

For example, the US dollar holds a distinction of high trust around the world as "fiat" money.

The 21st Century payroll deduction represents a hallmark of advancement in the personal management of money. One of the biggest blessings comes from having automatic savings, electronic bill pay, debit cards, on-line vacation reservations, and movie tickets as important currency transactions. As spenders, we are more directly involved in higher financial transaction levels than ever before.

The "spender tag" was one of Bernice's first realizations for change in her transformation from poor immigrant to stress-free, money-managing investor. Her Versace beach dress was purchased at a discount store. Understand: the majority of people with real net worth judiciously buy their things at a discount. We keep seeing that Women, Blacks, Latinos and other Americans struggling for positions of wealth **spend too much time shopping and not much time investing**.

Investor

Understand It As:
Someone who functions as an investigator and financial decision-maker of their own money, or capital, by putting it into business, real estate, stocks, bonds, currency trade, mutual funds, exchange-traded funds (ETFs), options, and retirement plans, etc. for the purpose of making a profit. Physical work is not necessarily involved in the making of the profit. They keep in mind that the risk of capital loss is always a possibility.

Risk tolerance is a cultural, psychological and financial set of preferences that we learn over time. Bernice took a very high risk in buying the almost defunct American Airlines (ARMQ) for just a few cents. She knew little about the process but could not believe that the "great, official American Airlines of the Caribbean", in a down market, cost so little. She realized that the company had real possible value at the penny price level. For three months, all of her available tip money went to buy ARMQ. The average price was .72 cents U.S. dollars per share. By the time she had 10,000 shares, she had accumulated a cost of $7,200. Later on, the market went up and she sold them at $6.42 per share, or at roughly $64,200! Yes, taxes were due, but SO WHAT?!

Risk for Bernice came in the simple idea that **money can buy possibly unnecessary junk or it can become "capital" and make even more money.** In Bernice's case, the money went out of her hands and, with GATO in mind of buying low and selling high, she sent it out with a bounce. Hence, it bounced back with a lot more.

> **Have a desire for a better lifestyle?**
>
> Do you want to get moving from just one paycheck to cash coming in on top of more sweet cash? Find yourself panicky by the process of earning money from investments? Search no further!
>
> <u>Fundamental Analysis Notes (FAN)</u> are here to help you earn real money. You get to enjoy a near-foolproof investment model:
>
> **First:** I describe a clear meaning for each key term that every investor must understand to make money.
>
> **Second:** I analyze various common techniques into a few, simple steps.
>
> **Third:** I honor different learning styles including visuals, hands-on learning, and solitary or group participations.
>
> So stop fretting, be smart! Learn how to make investment dollars.
>
> E-mail: segundo@segundoperez.org

Other more traditional, cultural risk preferences include low-risk investments that lead to conservative gains, such as certificates of deposit. Bond products of solid corporations and stable governments also make for safer, long-term investing. It may also include lending money to relatives or local non-proven businesses in an effort to "help the community". But look, investments are for making real money with the big girls and boys. We must play in the big leagues before we can even offer our financial services to those in the community who decide not to follow GATO. If you want to get all bent out of shape with me go ahead; I still love you! But with the way that things are structured in our communities, people tend to just spend, spend, and spend.

Investing in a car wash, for example, will put you to work, will make you sweat, and will also make you lose that hard earned money as soon as one of the primary investors or workers wants out. Forget small beauty shops or restaurants! They are slave-makers of the owner. Put your money into a national or international enterprise chain instead and gain that 3% to 5% constant quarterly gain, plus dividends. You will make money! You will prosper! You do not know about the 3% to 5% percent constant gain just yet. But you will later…

Bernice also invested in currencies. She understands tourism very well. Other investors may not feel comfortable doing the same thing. They may not invest in currencies because they decide to just learn about a few stocks and stay with them. The additional risk in currency investments is Bernice putting GATO to work and attempting to make a larger profit.

CREATING SUCCESSFUL STRATEGIES

• Think in outcomes rather than actions

• What result do you want from this goal?

• Purpose: Why do you want this result?

• Fundamental Analysis Notes (FAN)

Investors tend to hold a position in the same way. For a long time they may watch the investment and nurture it as it grows. Traders, on the other hand, buy and sell daily, weekly, or beyond. There are day traders, or "scalpers", that buy and sell in seconds with the help of computer programs. There are "swing traders" who follow the market to seek and trade investments according to how the market swings up or down over a few days. Finally, there are always a few who combine these efforts to balance their gain results. Ultimately, all are GATO money-making strategies.

**Intentional blank page for reader's notes:
[for Review in the form of reflection]**

CHAPTER 3.3

ASSURING LIVING WELL!

A new investor to the world of options or stock trading has one, and only one, thing to understand: do not jump until you know where you are landing. Yes, I am trying to warn you: "Personal business strategies are simple to execute ONCE you have taken the time to <u>read</u> and <u>learn</u> procedures for making guaranteed returns." The up and coming corporate executive risks exposure to failure without formal preparation and constant due diligence in her decision-making process. The small business owner risks bankruptcy by jumping into deals which do not serve the greater majority of money spending consumers, limiting sustainability over time.

You get a traffic ticket. Who is best to defend you? Yourself or that attorney that stuck every law book into her head and passed the state bar? I have a great cardiologist. I let that guy mess around with my heart because he studied it enough to pass the medical boards. The lawyer and the doctor both make a heck of a lot of money. Why? Because specialists read, study, and understand how to navigate the procedures needed to be successful in their fields. Trading, opening a business, or climbing corporate leadership can lead to excellent returns. Just remember: understand the knowledge, and especially the knowledge of GATO. These mechanisms will make you a successful specialist in transforming your personal financial experience.

A personal change is a risk. The question to always consider is: how MUCH risk can we handle? After attaining the proper motivation, business education, and spiritual understanding we can actually use change to reduce the risk in our life's business portfolio. Dr. Cheulho Lee, PhD., my finance professor at Florida Memorial University, hounded into his MBA students that if properly executed an opportunistic change in business strategy has the provability of obtaining less negative results than a corresponding "no change" position. He emphasized intrinsic value, constant involvement of fundamental analysis, hands-on awareness of the current economic environment, a quick strike trigger, and advantageous leverage as basic understandings for a successful, personal business life.

More Love, More Prosperity

Most Americans are not in poverty when defined in the context of being hungry, naked, and/or homeless. The real poverty among hard working people and their children is of being uncared for, unwanted, and unloved. We must restructure family life to avoid this type of poverty as an easy step to prosperity. Again, spread love rather than money wherever you go. Personal contact, regardless of the medium, ought to relay a happier experience than the person could have imagined. Inspire people to come to you because it will make them feel happier.

Love begins by taking care of the ones closest to home.

People hate to feel like they are nobodies. We cannot create our greatest empowered prosperity when we ourselves feel insignificant.

Lack of love whether for God, others, or yourself is much more difficult a bridge to rebuild on the great highway to prosperity than the learning of applications and financial strategies. Deliberate, holistic service becomes the ultimate self-experience of success for both ourselves and others. Prosperity is the net result of actions making up God's word, service to others, personal understanding, financial literacy, lifestyle and GATOS coming together in the joyous celebration of life.

All prosperous people understand what Mother Teresa stated: *"Let us more and more insist on raising funds of love, of kindness, of understanding, of peace. Money will come if we seek first the Kingdom of God… the rest will be given."*

More Focus on God-Guided Outcomes = More Prosperity

Prosperous people do not just do the work at hand for its sake, or profit, or because it has become a burdensome sentence of responsibility. We do it because our works are a direct, natural result of self-search for God's plan in our lives. He knows at what, how, when and where we can prosper best. Our job is to find it out, accept it, and execute it.

Take silent time in meditating prayer, though it is usually not part of the process for impulse expending. What is meditative prayer? It is a simple sharing of ideas, comparisons or thoughts with God, Jesus Christ, The Holy Spirit, Mother Mary, or a bunch of available Saints. Even just quiet time with one's self searching for a way to live a pious life leads to prosperity. We are not alone. We are who by choice made us alone. The answer is not Ma and Pa.

Now how are expenditures going to echo personal devotion to follow, serve, and live a life of spiritual faith with all that money? Again, a person in true prosperity carries a duty to still remain a "poor widow" in our stewardship life (Mark 12: 41-44). Choose not only to exist as in the life of the rich man (Mark 10:17-31). Remember: prosperity in flourishing good fortune, success, and all the joyful moments of life can only be real when accomplished in faith and an irrevocable partnership with Jesus Christ.

I wish you good luck on making additional money, whether it be from a new business venture, a promotion at work, or investments. Genuine success is the result of devotion, self-knowledge, preparation, and taking action over the right opportunity. "Motivate the Mind, Nourish the Spirit & Witness the Prosperity"… This is Living Money Bound!

END

ABOUT THE AUTHOR

Segundo Ramón Pérez Hernández is the creator of "Growth Action Thinking" total vision of personal success. He is a regular commentator on personal financial literacy. Individuals who attend his holistic seminar/workshops experience an expansion of hope for personal financial wellness.

www.ingramcontent.com/pod-product-compliance
Lightning Source LLC
LaVergne TN
LVHW051159080426
835508LV00021B/2702